TAORMINA AND NAXOS

PEARLS OF THE MEDITERRANEAN

EDIZIONI AFFINITÀ ELETTIVE

TAORMINA AND NAXOS
PEARLS OF THE MEDITERRANEAN

Love for this land is the common factor that binds all those who have contributed to the creation of this work. Thanks to Vincenzo Giusto, Bernard Michaud, Giuseppe Riggio, Sergio Todesco and Giuseppe Vitali. The painting on page 10 is taken from "La Sicilia dei viaggiatori", published by Maimone Editore.

Dedicated to Tiziana and Federica

AUTHOR: Rosaria Falcone

PHOTOGRAPHS AND ILLUSTRATIONS

Franco Barbagallo: pages 4, 38, 46.
Salvatore Centorrino: pages 42, 50, 54, 55, 78.
Domenico D'Arrigo: pages 51, 52.
Giangabriele Fiorentino: pages 3, 16, 17, 18, 24, 25, 27, 28, 29, 37, 45, 47, 49, 53, 58, 77.
Alfio Garozzo: pages 23, 32, 33, 44, 50, 54, 55, 56, 57, 58, 61, 67, 68, 72, 74, 87, 90, 93, 94.
Giuseppe Iacono: pages 48, 49.
Walter Leonardi: pages 14, 19, 41, 76, 77, 79.
Riccardo Lombardo: pages 64, 65, 69, 84.
Raimondo Marino: pages 23, 40, 76.
Leonardo R. Martignano: page 48.
Melo Minnella: pages 12, 21, 40, 78, 81, 84, 85.
Alessandro Saffo: pages 6, 7, 13, 17, 22, 31, 34, 36, 41, 43, 59, 63, 79.
Nino Statella: page 81.
Foto Tomarchio: pages 70, 71.
Antonio Zimbone: pages 15, 18, 20, 26, 28, 29, 75.

Cover photographs: Front **Alfio Garozzo**, Back **Raimondo Marino, Giangabriele Fiorentino, Alessandro Saffo, Alessandro Saffo.**

GRAPHICS: Claudio Falino
MAPS: "Legenda", la Cartografia di Novara
ENGLISH TRANSLATION: Nicholas Whithorn

Copyright by Società Editrice Affinità Elettive
via Saponara res. 13 - 98168 Messina - Italia
tel. 090.353107 pbx - fax 090.359443
Website: www.affinitaelettive.it • E-mail: affinitaelettive@hotmail.com

Welcome

Have you just arrived and don't know where to start? We have exactly the right solution for you.

Get hold of a comfortable pair of shoes, a swimming costume and a camera.

Add a little good company, a touch of curiosity and some good humour.

Wander through the narrow streets in the town centre, mix with the locals, dive into the beautiful crystal clear sea and sunbathe on the golden beaches.

Taormina is a town that offers you beaches and mountains, a place that will satisfy almost any desire you may have.

It is the most popular place for visitors in the whole province, a jewel in a setting of incomparable beauty, famous all over the world for its charm, its lively night life, its magnificent Greek theatre and its beautiful countryside.

Walking through the narrow streets of the pretty town, especially in the evening when they are lit up, is like walking in a dream or fairy story.

Bottom: Piazza IX Aprile. Facing page: panoramic view over the town.

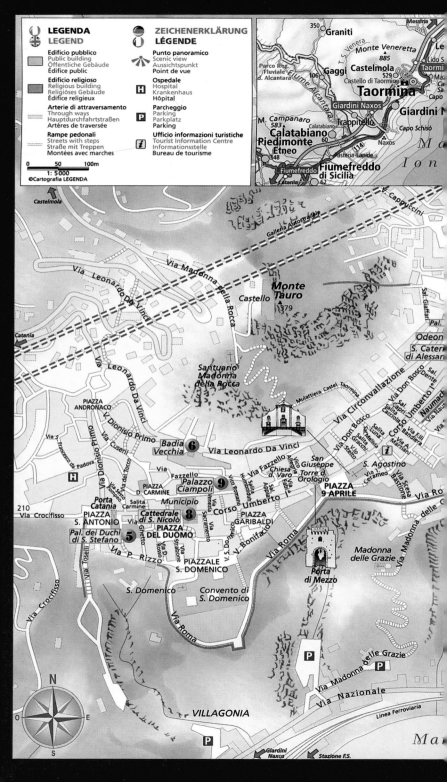

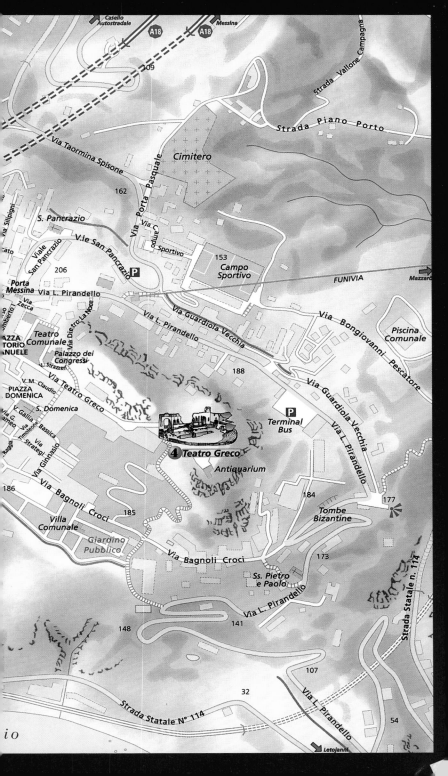

History

In 735BC the Athenian Theokles brought a group of settlers from Chalcis in Euboea and from the island of Naxos in the Cyclades and founded the first Greek colony in Sicily, giving it the name of Naxos.

The Sikels who lived in the area moved onto Monte Tauro, in the area where Taormina now stands.

The city of Naxos enjoyed a long period of peace and prosperity, thanks to farming and sheep-rearing, but in 403BC it was attacked and destroyed by Dionysius I, tyrant of Syracuse, as punishment for being allied with Athens. The inhabitants fled and some took

refuge on Monte Tauro. A few years later, in 392BC, Dionysius I, with the help of Imilcone's Carthaginians, overcame the resistance of the Sikels and enslaved many of the former citizens of Naxos.

358BC is generally considered the year in which the city of Tauromenion was founded by Andromachus, a Greek from Naxos, father of the historian Timaeus, who succeeded in getting rid of Dionysius I.

In 278BC the Greek Tindarione, who had taken military command of Tauromenion, made an alliance with Pyrrhus, King of Epirus, to defend the town from the Mamertines, mercenaries fighting under the orders of Syracuse. However, this alliance did not prevent

Bottom: painting by E. Lear from 1848 (private collection).

Agathocles, the new tyrant of Syracuse, from taking control of Tauromenion. Timeaus was exiled and lived the rest of his life in Athens.

In 212BC Tauromenion voluntarily subjected itself to Roman rule in order to gain protection against the threat posed by the Carthaginians and to avoid suffering the same fate as Syracuse, which had been destroyed by the Romans.

The town was given the name of Tauromoenium and became one of the first federated towns in Sicily, thus enjoying a certain degree of autonomy and some privileges, such as exemption from taxes. After a period of prosperity, at the end of the 1st century BC Octavian relegated Tauromoenium from the status of free city to that of Roman colony, forcing many of the inhabitants to leave and bringing in Roman settlers who were his political allies. From then until the fall of the Roman Empire in 476AD the life and economy of the town were heavily influenced by political and social upheavals. Under the rule of the Byzantine empire the town became the most important place in eastern Sicily because of its militarily strategic position. This led to considerable economic development and a sharp increase in the population. The town expanded southwards and the defensive walls, built in the Greek period, were doubled in some stretches.

In 902 Tauromoenium fell to the Arabs, who devastated the town, destroying houses and monuments and killing many of the inhabitants. In 962 the town was besieged again for a long time, again with the victory of the Arabs.

The name of the town was changed by Caliph Al Moez to Al-

Bottom: the Tauro fountain on an old postcard. Facing page: detail of the decoration of a Sicilian cart depicting Arabs and Normans fighting.

moezia. However, the Arabs did not bring only death and destruction. They also encouraged the development of agriculture by introducing new techniques and new crops, they stimulated the development of the sciences and philosophy and they left behind numerous words and expressions from their language.

The conquest of Sicily by the Normans put an end to the Arab domination.

In 1078 Count Roger conquered the town and restored its previous name. Under the Normans and the Swabians Tauromoenium experienced a renewed period of peace and prosperity, particularly during the reign of Frederick II.

The reign of the Angevins and the Aragonese, who fought each other in order to gain control of the Kingdom of the Two Sicilies, was characterised by the imposition of heavy taxation which led to a decline of the town's fortunes. In 1409 the first meeting of the Sicilian Parliament was held in Taormina in order to nominate a successor to Martin II, King of Sicily, who died without heirs. Martin I, designated to replace his son, left effective control of the kingdom to his daughter-in-law, Bianca di Navarra. The Spanish kept possession of the Island until 1713, when Sicily passed for a short time into the hands of the Savoias, with Vittorio Amedeo II, and then to the Hapsburgs of Austria. From 1734 onwards, Sicily returned to Spanish rule with Charles III of Bourbon.

Naxos had been nothing more than the port of Taormina throughout mediaeval times, but in this period it developed as a rural village of citrus fruit growers and became known as the "garden village", hence the current name of Giardini Naxos.

In 1860, Sicily was liberated from the Bourbons. Garibaldi's troops arrived in Taormina in August of that year; Garibaldi then set sail for Calabria from the bay of Naxos.

Visiting the Town

It is generally recognised that it was the Germans who set in motion the tourist industry in Taormina. Already in the 1700s German writers gained their inspiration from the charming atmosphere of the town, German artists painted the picturesque countryside, German travellers wrote their diaries and German poets composed verses on the beauty of the place. One of these was the great Goethe, who arrived in Taormina in 1787 and recorded his impressions in his diary Journey through Italy.

The long list of famous people who have helped to bring Taormina to prominence also includes the artist Otto Geleng, who reproduced the beautiful landscape of the area in his canvases in 1863, to great critical acclaim.

A few years later Wilhelm von Gloeden, an eccentric character from a noble family, immortalised Taormina in artistic photographs published all over Europe, creating a great deal of interest. From the late 1800s onwards the French, Americans and English joined the Germans in the streets of Taormina.

In the 1900s rich heiresses in search of adventure flirted with young local men, causing scandal and gossip. Undoubtedly the air of Taormina brought to life hidden passions: even the famous D.H. Lawrence was intoxicated with the town and while he was here

found the inspiration to write his famous novel Lady Chatterley's Lover, which caused so much scandal on its publication.

In the 1950s the dietician Hauser (another German) received his important clients in his villa: famous actresses, artists and writers who, perhaps, found it easier to follow the strict diets he imposed on them contemplating the beautiful Taormina sunsets.

Today Taormina is

an exceptional holiday destination, famous all over the world; today's visitors experience the same emotions, the same electrifying and, at the same time, sensual atmosphere.

If you want to fully appreciate the beauty of Taormina, the best times of year to visit are spring and autumn, when the air is warm and fragrant and the main tourist season is yet to start or has already finished.

Taormina is an aristocratic town sitting on its 250 metre high hilltop and overlooking a crystal clear blue sea; Etna in the background, distant but forbiddingly ever present, as if offering you unforgettable emotions. Alleyways and picturesque courtyards, artistic arches and stairways, surprises round every corner: wandering slowly around the town is the best way of visiting it, admiring its beauty and soaking up the atmosphere.

Top: Catania Gate.

If, however, you want a more systematic tour of the town, in order not to miss anything, we suggest the following itinerary.

You enter the centre of Taormina, from the south, through the Catania Gate (also called del Tocco), situated in the defensive walls. It was restored in the Aragonese period and is surmounted by an aedicule, framed by columns, bearing the Aragonese coat of arms and the date 1440. The Catania Gate marks the southern boundary of the old Town, the heart of Taormina and the area containing numerous examples of 15th century architecture.

Near the Gate, in via De Spuches, stands the massive structure of the Palazzo dei Duchi di Santo Stefano, once belonging to the De Spuches family, Princes of Galati and Dukes of Santo Stefano. The original building, probably dating from the 13th cen-

tury, incorporated part of the pre-existing defensive walls of the town. It was built in Gothic style and also included elements in clear Arab-Norman style: the elegant two-mullioned windows, decorated with rose windows and trefoil arches; the swallow-tailed battlements; the serrated crowning frieze, made with alternate layers of black lava stone and white Siracusa stone, creating a magnificent effect. The same alternation of black and white can be seen in the façade and in the portal leading to the reception room on the ground floor, characterised by a high vaulted ceiling with a central column. In the small garden you will see an old well. The building is now home to the Mazzullo Foundation and inside you can see a display of works by the sculptor Giuseppe Mazzullo (1913-1988) and archaeological artefacts.

Top: Palazzo dei Duchi di Santo Stefano.

Bottom: two-mullioned window in Palazzo dei Duchi di Santo Stefano.

Further along via De Spuches you turn left into via Pietro Rizzo, which leads to the small San Domenico square, where you will find the ex-Monastery of Saint Dominic. The building dates from the 14th century and was originally a fortified palace belonging to the Prince of Cerami, Damiano Rosso, who became a monk and donated it to the Dominicans. In the 1900s the Princes of Cerami retook possession of the building and decided to turn it into a hotel. Today, the San Domenico Palace Hotel is one of the most prestigious and best known ho-

tels in Italy. The monks' cells of the old monastery are now luxurious rooms for the hotel guests and you can still see some of the original furniture of the monastery , as well as the charming 17th century cloister with its arched columns. The adjacent Church of Saint Agatha collapsed during the Second World War but you can still see the bell tower (17th-18th century) and, inside the hotel congress hall, the remains of the altars.

From the San Domenico square you can turn into the panoramic via Roma, which will lead you to the Municipal Park, named after Duke Giovanni Colonna di Cesarò. Apart from offering you the opportunity of relaxing in the shade of the numerous trees, from the park you will get a magnificent view of the coastline below, from Giardini Naxos to Acireale. Inside the park there is a curious pagoda shaped construction, which was built at the end of the 19th

Top: San Domenico Palace Hotel.

Bottom: Municipal Park.

century. Also from the San Domenico square, you can go up the stairway which leads to Piazza Duomo, where you will find the Cathedral, dedicated to Saint Nicholas of Bari. It was built in the late 15th century on the site of a pre-existing mediaeval church and has undergone numerous al-

On this page, from the top: Cathedral of Saint Nicholas and Tauro fountain, detail of the 15th century portal, interior of the Cathedral.
Facing page, top: detail of the Tauro fountain.

terations and extensive restoration work over the centuries. Its present appearance is that of an imposing fortress-church, thanks particularly to the crowning battlements. The façade has an attractive baroque portal with a split tympanum flanked by columns, two interesting 15th century single-lancet windows and, high up, a small 16th century rose window. The two side portals of the Cathedral are particularly interesting: the one on Corso Umberto I is 15th century, decorated by a plait of floral motifs and framed in lava stone, while the one on the right hand side is 16th century.

Inside the layout is that of a Latin cross with three naves divided by pink marble columns. There are numerous works of art, most importantly including a panel polypytch by Antonello de Saliba portraying the "Virgin with Child, Saints Girolamo and Sebastian, la Our Lady of Mercy and Saints Lucy and Agatha" (1504) and a statue of Our Lady with Child attributed to Gagini (16th century). There

Top: Palazzo Ciampoli.

Facing page: the Badia Vecchia.

are two interesting small chapels on either side of the church. In front of the Cathedral you can see the artistic Tauro Fountain, so called because on top it has the figure of a biped female centaur which has become the civic emblem of Taormina. The fountain was created in 1635 in late mannerist style and stands on a base of three steps; the basins are richly decorated with mythological figures, sea creatures and putti.

On the opposite side of Piazza Duomo is the Town Hall, with its attractive 17th century windows on the second floor.

If you follow the road downhill to the right of the square, you come to the façade of a building known as Casa Floresta. You will notice the Gothic portal and the 16th century windows. In the interior courtyard there is an external staircase leading to the first floor.

Returning onto Piazza Duomo, slightly uphill from Corso Umberto stands the massive construction of the so called Badia Vecchia, which owes its peculiar castle keep shape to its Norman origins. Its later adaptation to a noble residence and the inclusion of late Gothic decorative motifs date from the 14th century. In particular, you will notice the two coloured frieze, created by using white Siracusa stone and black lava stone, and, above this, a series of three splendid ogival two-mullioned windows. On each side, the building is crowned by swallow-tailed battlements.

*Bottom:
Clocktower.*

Returning onto Corso Umberto, a little further on from Piazza Duomo, on the left you come to Palazzo Ciampoli, at the top of a wide staircase. The lower of the two floors has an attractive portal decorated with vigorous profiles in relief in the two top corners; it dates from 1412, as can be seen from the coat of arms in the diamond above the portal. The upper floor has two-mullioned windows and was built in the late 15th century. A second portal gives access to the interior courtyard, which is overlooked by the windows of the rooms, a typical Arab architectural style which is widespread in Sicily. Today the building is one of the prettiest hotels in Taormina.

Returning once more onto the Corso, where there is a series of buildings with architecturally interesting elements (such as the 15th century portal of Geleng house), another stairway to the left, via D'Orville, leads up to the Varo Church or Church of the Visitation dating from the late 17th century. Inside you can see some interesting works of art: a 14th century painted Cross, by an unknown artist, and paintings by Tuccari, particularly a fresco behind the high altar portraying the Triumph of the Cross. Behind the church there is a crypt which predates the building.

Continuing along Corso Umberto I you come to the Clock Tower, which marks the end of the old town. The Tower was built in the 12th century, probably

on pre-existing foundations from the Greek period, and it encompasses the so-called Halfway Gate; the clock was inserted during the rebuilding work in 1679, which gave the Tower its present form.

After passing the Halfway Gate, you turn into the panoramic Piazza IX Aprile, where it is worth stopping a while to enjoy the spectacular view of Mount Etna. In this square you will find the ex-Church of Saint Augustine, now home to the Municipal Library.

It was built in 1486 in honour of Saint Sebastian, who, according to popular tradition, saved the town from the threat of the plague. It later became the property of the Augustans, who extended it and named it after Saint Augustine.

Over the centuries the building has undergone extensive alterations and little remains of the original structure, except for a small rose window in the façade and the upper part of the portal.

The bell tower is decorated with battlements and arches framed in lava stone.

On the opposite side of the square, at the top of beautiful stairway with balustrades, stands the Church of Saint Joseph, which was built in the late 17th century. The pyramid

Top: ex Church of Saint Augustine in the picturesque Piazza IX Aprile.

Bottom: attractive mosaic in the Mezzo Gate.

23

shaped façade is characterised by the baroque portal and, high up, a niche with a statue of Christ. Alongside the façade is the elegant bell tower with a multifoiled spire. The interior is in Latin cross shape and contains an ossuary, marked by a marble slab on the floor, and some interesting 17th century canvases depicting episodes from the life of Mary.

Further along Corso Umberto I you come to an alleyway leading to the so-called Naumachiae, one of the most important examples of Imperial Roman architecture in Sicily.

It was uncovered from 1943 onwards and consists of a huge water tank surrounded by a brick wall 122 metres in length, probably intended to hold water flowing in from other tanks; later it was probably used for other purposes, maybe even as a gymnasium.

Bottom: the Naumachiae, architectural remains from the Imperial Roman period in Sicily.

Along the length of the wall there is a series of 18 large apsidal niches, which maybe once housed statues, and small rectangular niches of the style used in decorative fountains. In the area in front of the Naumachiae remains of mosaics from Roman

houses have been uncovered, as well as the ancient floor in lava stone. At the end of Corso Umberto stands the splendid Palazzo Corvaja, which overlooks Piazza Vittorio Emanuele II.

This complex and stylish building belongs to three different historical periods: the Arabs built a cubic shaped military tower on top of ruins from the Greek period; in the 13th century the main body of the building, called the "Salone del Maestro Giustiziere", to the left of the entrance portal was added; finally, in the early 15th century the part of the building overlooking the square was built, with four two-mullioned windows on the first floor resting on an attractive coloured frieze. The south-western façade is characterised by a single three-mullioned window and a portal leading into the courtyard with an exterior staircase climbing up to the first floor.

The large hall in the 15th century wing of the building was used for the meeting of the Sicilian Parliament on 25th September 1411. in the 16th century the whole complex became the property of the Corvaja family; today it houses the "Museum of Sicilian Arts and Traditions Panarello Collection", which exhibits a large collection of art and craft objects dating from the 16th to the 20th centuries.

In the Greek period the present day Piazza Vittorio Emanuele II was the Agora, the main square of Tauromoenion, situated at the junction of the two principal streets, the 'consolare Valeria' (now Corso Umberto) and the decumano (now via Teatro Greco). This was the heart of the town, where the assemblies of the town council and the markets were held and where the most important public buildings were located.

This square also housed the Roman Forum from 201BC onwards.

On one side of the square, corresponding to via Timeo and Palazzo Corvaja, there was a Hellenistic Temple which was periptero (with a cella surrounded by a continuous line of columns), dating from the 2nd century BC, probably dedicated to Dionysus.

You can still see part of the three stepped base (stylobàtes) and the marks left by the bases of the

Top and bottom: Palazzo Corvaja.

continued on page 28

The Museum of Art and Popular Traditions in Palazzo Corvaja

The museum collection housed in Palazzo Corvaja (10th-15th century) consists of an extraordinary variety of objects, of great artistic value and extremely important in the understanding of the development of popular figurative culture in Sicily. All the material on display in the "Sicilian Museum of Art and Popular Traditions" is privately owned and offers important evidence of the cultural and historical events that took place in the 'privileged' environment of Taormina during the first seventy years of the last century. In other words, we are talking about the Taormina of Baron Wilhelm von Gloeden and Roger Peyrefitte, of D.H. Lawrence and the Nazi party officials, but also the Taormina of Luchino Visconti and of Hollywood stars, and the Taormina which Antonino Uccello visited during the 1960s in his untiring search for objects relating to the popular traditions of Sicily.

Several years ago it was decided to make the most of this collection and open it to the public in order to help preserve the historical memory of this important period in the civil and cultural history, not only of Taormina, but of the whole of Sicily. This would not have been possible without the help of the owner of the collection, the antique dealer and collector Giovanni Panarello, a figure who is a unique mixture of patron, host and aesthete and still today represents an important source of knowledge about the life and culture

Bottom: courtyard of Palazzo Corvaja.

of the people of Taormina over the last sixty years. Panarello is a man of great aesthetic taste who had the good fortune to find these various objects of popular art when they were still part and parcel of the everyday life of the period. His skill and vision lie in the fact that he could look forward and see that these objects would have an important figurative and documentary value in the future.

The Museum is open every day and houses a collection (about 500 objects) of great ethno-anthropological interest, including

objects of great rarity and beauty, showing the forms taken by figurative popular art in Sicily over the last three centuries. These range from the anatomic and painted votive offerings (the latter are copies dating from the 1950s, but are in charming naïf style) to the paintings on glass, from devotional statues (Saints, Baby Jesus and Our Lady in wood, papier-mâché, alabaster, wax and other materials) to pottery (large decorated plates, holy water fonts, 18th-19th century oil lamps in human figure shapes). There are also singular large oil portraits of typical Sicilian people and family groups, lacework, objects made by shepherds (kegs and water flasks, distaffs and shuttles, pickets and carved wooden collars, drinking horns etc.), puppets, models of Sicilian carts, wax models, nativity scenes (made of wax, terracotta, ivory, mother-of-pearl and other materials). Some of the curious pieces, worthy of note for their archaic beauty, are a wooden ex voto (Our Lady with Child) and numerous scale models of processional "varette" (the litters on which statues of Saints are carried) with the relative Saints, all 19th and 20th century works by shepherds from the north-east of Sicily. The exhibition is presently simple and elementary; the curator, Franz Riccobono, is currently working on a series of explanatory material setting out the artistic and cultural context of the various objects on display. Over the last fifty years Taormina has experienced the gradual, and in some cases traumatic, move from elite tourism, within which the whole area was considered as a picturesque natural environment, to mass tourism, with its emphasis on the "consumption" of the area's heritage. The Museum of Palazzo Corvaja represents a valid alternative to this confused and hurried approach to tourism: a visit to this collection could represent a sort of introduction to the "genius loci" of Taormina..

Sergio Todesco

continued from page 25

Top: the three-mullioned window of Palazzo Corvaja and the Church of Saint Catherine of Alexandria.

Bottom: the Odeon Theatre.

columns, which are visible inside the Church of Saint Catherine.

Right next to this temple a small Odeon or theatre was built in the Imperial Roman age, using one side of the temple as the backdrop to the stage. The Odeon copied the architectural layout of classical theatres, with a cavea, stage and orchestra; it differed from the main Theatre in terms of size (it could house only 200 spectators), of location, being situated in the heart of the town, and of orientation

(it faces north-east while the main Theatre faces south). The typical semi-circular shaped theatre was built of clay bricks and had five wedge shaped sectors of seats. It was probably used for poetry recitals or musical performances put on for the benefit of the most important members of the community. All that remains of the Odeon are the walls that supported the stage and the ruins of a small room used by the actors. In front of the Odeon stands the Church of St. Catherine of Alexandria, built in the late 17th century. The façade is characterised by an 18th century portal

decorated with volutes and putti, above which there is a niche containing a statue of Saint Catherine created in 1705 by Paolo Greco.

Inside the church, apart from the remains of the Hellenistic Temple visible under the floor, you can admire a 16th century panel painting; an 18th century wooden Crucifix on the altar to the right; a statue of Saint Catherine dating from the late 1400s; a panel painting depicting the martyrdom of the Saint, painted by Jacopo Vi-

Via Teatro Greco and its countless souvenir and local craftwork shops.

29

gnerio in the 16th century. Near the northern side of the Forum (Piazza Vittorio Emanuele) the remains of the Roman Spa (1st-2nd century AD) have been uncovered. This complex consisted of a frigidarium, tepidarium and calidarium (pools for cold, warm and hot baths); the remains can be seen behind the Congress Hall.

From the Piazza you can go uphill along via Teatro Greco to reach the Greek-Roman Theatre, the largest ancient theatre in Sicily after the one in Siracusa (open to visitors every day from 9 a.m. un-

til one hour before sunset). Next to the Theatre you can visit a small Antiquarium housing artefacts of various origins: epigraphs, carvings and pieces recovered from the various monuments of Taormina. There is a particularly interesting torso of Apollo from the Hellenistic age and numerous tablets documenting details of the administrative and political life of the Greek town.

Going back the way you came, towards Piazza Vittorio Emanuele,

continued on page 40

The Greek Theatre

During the period in which Syracuse was governed by Hieron II, Tauromoenion enjoyed a certain degree of autonomy and, despite the heavy taxation imposed by the tyrant, experienced a period of great wealth and splendour, as is testified by the completion of important public works. For the building of the theatre a site with a magnificent view was chosen.

Above the theatre there was a temple dedicated to Apollo archagètas, of which only the base remains.

Apollo archagètas was the guide and counsellor of Theocles when he arrived in Sicily and founded Naxos and the people of Tauromoenion were devoted to him.

With a little imagination you can relive the atmosphere of that era, picturing yourself together with the polis (people), watching the tragedies of Aeschylus, Sophocles and Euripides or the comedies of Aristophanes, all against the magnificent backdrop of the bay of Naxos and Mount Etna.

In the "parascenium" on the right (the part of stage structure jutting out to the side), built later by the Romans, you can still see four blocks of Taormina stone on which four Greek words are engraved: iereia (priestess), iereian (religion), and – repeated twice – Filistous, a Greek name typical of Taormina which still exists today in the altered form of Filistad. The theatre was built in a depression in the hillside and was originally in accordance with the standard Greek architecture, consisting of an orchestra, a cavea and a stage, like the one in Syracuse; the maximum diameter of the theatre is 109 metres, that of the orchestra is 35 metres.

Unusually, the theatre faces southwards: usually, this position was avoided so as not to expose the spectators to the heat of the sun. In this case the unusual choice is due to various reasons: first of all, the terrace on which the town stood was to the south of the hill housing the theatre and the brow of the hill was useful as defence for the northern side. The theatre couldn't face away from the town, otherwise people would have had to walk around the outside of the hill to get to the top, passing through the area between the walls, an exposed area in the case of military action; moreover, building the theatre according to traditional practice would have meant reducing the steepness of the hill, which was useful for defence purposes. Another, no less important reason, was that the spectators would not have been able to enjoy the spectacular view as a background to the performances. With their love of all things grandiose and colossal, the Romans completely changed the appearance of the theatre which had been designed and built by the Greeks of Tauromoenion.

Firstly, they built the large semicircular portico surrounding the "summa cavea", the monumental stage and the two wings to the side of the stage.

Later, they turned the orchestra into an arena for the "ludi gladiatori" by building the "podium", in other words the semicircular covered corridor that runs around the orchestra and separates it from the bottom of the cavea, indispensable in order to protect the public from the dangers of this kind of spectacle. Above the podium were the seats reserved for the most important magistrates of the town and guests of honour. Under the stage you can still see the drainage system for rainwater, without which the stage and the orchestra would have flooded. The drainage system is in a T shape. The horizontal line is under the orchestra, while the vertical line passes under the wall of the stage, across the floor of the covered corridor behind the stage and, finally, disgorges the water onto the hillside. This drainage system was also used to create steam, which was used for special effects when divinities appeared during the performances.

The stage was fixed and represented the façade of a two storey building. According to expert opinion, it was decorated with two levels of columns, one on top of the other; the lower level was made up of a series of nine granite columns, three groups of three columns at an equal distance from one another; the upper level was made up of 18 smaller granite columns, also an equal distance from one another.

The columns on the stage were in Corinthian style, characterised

by capitals decorated with laurel leaves sculpted in relief.

Apart from the two levels of columns, the stage was characterised by three large arched openings at an equal distance from one another.

The "porticus post scena" was a large colonnaded courtyard, a meeting place for the spectators. Next to the stage there are two wings, large rooms in which the actors changed or rested between scenes. The orchestra is the open area low down in the centre, dividing the stage from the cavea. In the Greek period the orchestra, housed the musicians who accompanied the performance of the tragedy or the comedy; in the Roman period it was also used as an

Bottom: the Greek Theatre with Naxos and Etna in the background.

arena. The cavea consists of the tiers of seats which rose up from the level of the orchestra to the top of the theatre (summa cavea), widening as they rose. All the seats of the cavea were covered with slabs of marble 2 centimetres thick.

The cavea was divided horizontally by five communication aisles – called "diazomata" by the Greeks and "praecinctiones" by the Romans, in other words fenced zones – along which spectators passed on their way to their seats.

The cavea was also crossed perpendicularly by 8 narrow stairways ("vomitoria"), which divided it into nine wedges, allowing the spectators to reach the sector of seating in which their places were situated.

If you consider, moreover, the junctions between the three horizontal aisles and the eight perpendicular stairways, without considering the aisle at the bottom of the cavea and the one at the top, each wedge was divided into four smaller wedges, making a total of 36 wedges.

This division of the cavea into 36 sectors made it easy for spectators to find their seats.

The acoustics were, and still are, perfect. The shape of the theatre creates a sort of soundbox, making it easy to hear clearly what is said on the stage from anywhere you are sitting.

The "summa cavea" was closed off by a semicircular wall which had eight openings leading into the "vomitoria", connecting the cavea with the double corridor situated behind the wall.

On the inside of the wall, divided into nine sections by the eight openings, there were four niches in each section, creating a harmonious decorative effect. They housed statues or vases.

The semicircular wall also served as a pediment supporting the columns holding up the ceiling of the first covered corridor. There were 5 columns in each section, making a total of 45 columns. With the 27 columns on the stage there were 72 columns in all, with their relative bases and capitals. Today, only 4 remain on the stage, placed there when the theatre was restored in 1860.

The two corridors surrounding the "summa cavea" were connected by stairs. Above the roofs of the two corridors there were two terraces, also semicircular, which housed wooden seats for the women, who had to be separated from the men during performances, in accordance with the "lex Julia" promulgated by Emperor Augustus Octavius to preserve levels of morality.

The function of the two large corridors was to allow the spectators to shelter from the rain or to take a stroll during the intervals. The two large terraces above the wings and the portico behind the stage had the same function.

The central part of the stage was probably destroyed during the Arab invasion of 902.

During the Arab occupation houses were built inside the theatre and remained there until the early 19th century, as can be seen from drawings made of the theatre by the French archaeologists Jean Houel and Saint-Non between 1781 and 1787.

The extraordinary beauty of the theatre and the incomparable scenery of the bay of Naxos, dominated by Etna, fascinated Frederick II, who transformed the structure to the right of the stage into an imperial palace. The Emperor welcomed important dignitaries and friends in the theatre itself; the theatre also became the residence of his first wife Constance of Aragon.

Over the centuries, this palace inside the theatre passed from one family to another.

The marble covering the cavea was removed and used, in part, in the construction of the Cathedral; all the columns, except for 4, were removed elsewhere.

Taormina and its ever more dilapidated theatre lost their former splendour and were forgotten until the 1700s, when artists and writers rediscovered it and brought it back into the limelight through their works.

Bernard Michaud

continued from page 31

and continuing to follow Corso Umberto you come to Messina Gate, originally part of the mediaeval defensive walls ands rebuilt in 1808. After passing through the gate you find yourself in Largo Giove Serapide, where you will

Top: Messina Gate.

see the Church of Saint Pancras, dedicated to the patron of the town who, according to legend, was stoned to death in Taormina when he came here to preach the Gospel. The church was built in the second half of the 17th century on top of the ruins of a Greek temple from the Hellenistic age, dedicated to Jupiter serapide. The large blocks of stone in the exterior walls of the church are from this temple. To either side of the 18th century portal with Ionic columns are statues of Saint Pancras and Saint Procopio. Inside there are 18th century paintings and a statue of Saint Pancras decorated in gold. If you feel like going a little further, away from the normal tourist areas, Taormina has other surprises to offer. On via Pirandello, which leads all the way down from the centre of Taormina to the coast offering breathtaking views, you can stop off to admire the

Above: digs in largo Giove Serapide.

Bottom: Church of Saint Pancras.

view or to take a few photos from the Belvedere ('beautiful view' in Italian, a very appropriate name). Further down the hill there is a necropolis called Colombario, because it is composed of small cells lying on top of one another, dating back to a period between

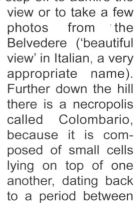

the 9th and 11th century. Near the Colombario, at the junction of via Pirandello and via Bagnoli Croce, stands the ex-Convent of Santa Maria del Gesù, built in the 13th century and of considerable interest because of its 16th century cloister, which is entered through

a portal dating from the same period. It is also worth seeing the colourful baptismal font situated in the sacristy.

On the road leading up to Castelmola there is a turn-off that leads to the Sanctuary of Our Lady of the Rock.

Near the Sanctuary, a stairway leads up to the ruins of the Medieval Castle, built on the summit of Monte Tauro (400m) on the site of the acropolis of the ancient town. All that remains of the castle are an isolated tower on the edge of a precipice, probably used as a lookout tower, an underground passageway and a tank used to collect rainwater. You can also see traces of terraces and stairs and other ruins. You can reach the castle by climbing the stairway starting a few hundred metres from Largo Giove Serapide: a healthy walk worth the effort in order to enjoy the magnificent view.

If you want to get a view from even higher up, you can continue along the road leading to Castelmola, a pretty little town just four kilometres from Taormina. Along the way, before reaching the town, you can see the Necropolis of Cocolonazzo of Mola, with cave tombs dating back to the a period between the 10th and 7th centuries BC.

Top: panoramic view of the Letojanni coastline.

Bottom: panoramic view of the town of Taormina.

Castelmola

Castelmola is situated at a height of 550 metres above sea level on the site of the primitive defensive settlement founded by the Sikels in the 8th century BC. Piazza S. Antonio is a panoramic viewpoint overlooking the coast below and is the heart of the town. A stairway to the right of the Piazza leads to the highest part of Castelmola, where you will find the ruins of the 16th century Castle. The area occupied by the castle is now a war memorial park. Also leading off Piazza S. Antonio is via Tutti i Santi, which will take you to the old Church of Saint George, built in the 17th century, with a façade containing a small bell compartment. Turning into via San Giorgio you come to the Parish Church of Saint Nicholas of Bari. It was rebuilt in 1935 but the side portal, a beautiful carved wooden pulpit and the altars are from the original building. It houses some interesting works of art.

Facing page: Church of Saint George.
Bottom: the Castle.

Before leaving Castelmola, we recommend stopping off for a drink at the bar San Giorgio and paying a visit to the workshop run by Francesco D'Agostino, in via De Gasperi, where you can admire and purchase the objects he makes from the trunk of the ferula, a common plant in Sicily.

Refined pottery and craftwork from the souvenir shops in Castelmola.

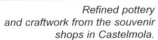

45

The sea at Taormina's feet

Along with the many other attractions Taormina offers you the chance of getting to the beach in just a few minutes.

The coastline at the foot of the town has something for everyone: sandy or pebble beaches of all shapes and sizes, quiet cliffs, charming bays and spectacular rocky outcrops, caves to explore and, above all, a crystal clear inviting sea both above and below the water.

While everybody can admire the cliffs and stacks, divers have the added pleasure of discovering an underwater world full of caves and gorges.

Coming down from Taormina towards the coast and turning left along the main SS 114 road, you come to Cape Sant'Andrea, where there are some lovely grottos that can be visited on board small boats, such as the superb grotta azzurra. A boat trip is the best way of viewing the rocky coastline, which is otherwise rather inaccessible.

After Cape Sant'Andrea there is a series of sandy beaches with bathing establishments, very popular with tourists: Spisone, Mazzarò – opposite which you can admire the luxuriant island of Isola Bella – connected to Taormina by a cable car.

Immediately after Mazzarò, after another stretch of rocky coastline, is the beach of Letojanni, a pleasant town overlooking a magnificent bay, which offers visitors interesting cultural and artistic events all year round. The mild seaside climate, the luxuriant

continued on page 50

Facing page: panoramic view of the beach of Giardini-Naxos. Bottom: the sea below Taormina.

Isola Bella

The Isola Bella Nature reserve has been in operation since 1999 and is run by the WWF.

It includes Capo Sant'Andrea, the Isola Bella and the entire facing coastline.

This rocky islet is covered with luxuriant Mediterranean vegetation and has become a landmark of Taormina.

It is connected to the land by a

sandy isthmus.

The reserve is home to plants of considerable interest with some endemic species, such as the white cabbage, the Ionic limonium and the Taormina cornflower

The wildlife includes the peregrine falcon and the blue rock thrush, as well as numerous species of seabirds, such as the cormorant, the black-headed gull and the herring gull.

The reserve can be visited all year round by appointment.

continued from page 46

Mediterranean vegetation and the groves of lemon trees all go to make Letojanni a popular tourist destination.

Further on, finally, you reach the beach of Cape Sant'Alessio, at the foot of a promontory with a castle. Off the coastline of Cape Sant'Alessio several shipwrecks have been found, along with their loads of amphorae.

Top and bottom: the long beach of Letojanni. Left: Cathedral.
Facing page: Capo Sant'Alessio.

Sant'Alessio Siculo and Forza D'Agro'

Sant'Alessio Siculo is overlooked by Cape Sant'Alessio with its Castle, which was built in Norman times on the site of previously existing fortifications dating from the Roman era. Sant'Alessio Siculo is a lively town, very popular with tourists because of its beautiful beach and convenient position.

You should visit the Villa Genovese and the Mezzo district, the oldest part of the town full of buildings dating from the 17th and 18th centuries.

If you happen to be in the area around Easter or Christmas be sure

Top: the Castle of Sant'Alessio. Bottom: Punta Sant'Alessio. Facing page: town and beach of Sant'Alessio.

Facing page, top: statue of Nike.

Bottom: the attractive waiting room in Giardini Naxos railway station.

to try the 'cuddure' or the 'crispelle', typical local cakes made and eaten at these times of year.

A lot of women in Sant'Alessio continue to keep alive the art of embroidery; it is easy to find works of embroidery to be bought as attractive souvenirs of your trip.

Above Cape Sant'Alessio, just four kilometres away, stands Forza d'Agrò, situated at a height of 400 metres above sea level on the slopes of the Peloritani mountains. This old town (the name is an abbreviation of the word fortress) was founded and expanded in Norman times around the Basilian monastery and the castle, the remains of which dominate the town and the coastline from on high. Forza d'Agrò is a mediaeval town and still has the characteristic narrow streets that make it so picturesque.

The Castle can be reached by climbing a stairway and the parts that can still be seen are the outer walls, some of the internal walls, the entrance gate and the walkway above it. The Castle was connected to a fortified watchtower with slits by an underground passage, allowing soldiers to move safely to and fro.

It is also worth visiting the Church of the Triad and the adjacent ex-monastery, which houses works of art from the Antonello school, as well as the Cathedral, built in the 15th century. The present day façade of the Cathedral dates from the 18th century restoration and has an interesting 16th century portal. The interior consists of three naves and houses interesting 17th and 18th century paintings, as well as a cross attributed to Antonello da Messina.

Other buildings of interest include the 15th century Durazzesca Gate and the Church of Saint Francis.

Giardini Naxos

If, on the other hand, you turn right after leaving Taormina, you come to the lovely sandy bay of Giardini-Naxos, situated between Cape Taormina and Cape Schisò. It was from here, in 1860, that Garibaldi set sail for Calabria, as you will see from the monument commemorating this event. Giardini-Naxos is a town with numerous facilities for tourists and hosts several important artistic and cultural events during the year. It is famous for its large sandy beach and the archaeological site of the ancient town of Naxos.

Naxos: the first Greek colony in Sicily

A bronze statue of Nike with an epigraph by Quasimodo commemorates the landing of the Chalcidians at Cape Schisò. Naxos was founded in this area in 735BC. Recent excavations have allowed archaeologists to get a good idea of the size and layout of the town when it was founded and its later development.

At the end of the 8th century BC the town covered an area of about ten hectares, just inland from the Bay of Schisò, where the oldest fragments of pottery have been found. This older part of the town contained numerous sacred buildings.

Recently, the site of a suburban Sanctuary has been uncovered. This was separated from the town by the Santa Venera river and had three cellae, probably belonging to three separate connecting buildings dedicated to different divinities.

It has so far been impossible to identify which divinities were worshipped here; the only clue available is an inscription referring to the warrior god Enyò.

The archaic cellae are very simple structures without colonnades, consisting of brick walls on stone bases; the roof and tympanum were decorated with layers of painted clay and terracotta objects: numerous fragments of decorations, Gorgon and sphinx masks have been found around the cellae.

A Necropolis was found near the northern edge of the town and the shoreline in 1980. So far about 400 tombs have been brought to

Bottom: watchtower.

light, some of which were on top of one another, probably indicating that they belonged to members of the same family. The tombs contain bodies buried in the ground or in pithoi (large containers originally used for foodstuffs). There is evidence of the production of vases, bowls and craters in clay during the archaic period, all made using local raw materials.

In the 7th century BC the town already covered the whole lava stone platform of the Schisò peninsula. The surviving traces of the streets dating from this period bear witness to the existence of various districts laid out in different ways; the most important streets appear to be those crossing the town in a north-south direction and leading to the coastline. The Sanctuary discovered on the south-western edge of the town, at the meeting point of the two stretches of walls to the right of the entrance to the archaeological site, dates back to the end of the 7th century BC.

The thémenos (sacred enclosure) was made up of high walls of lava stone blocks with rounded edges – according to a custom widely used in Greece but rarely in the western colonies – and had galleries (propilei) linking it to the town and the sea. Within the enclosure there are also the ruins of a sacred building on top of which in a later period, perhaps the 5th century BC, a larger Temple was built. You

Top: remains of the buildings of the Greek colony of Naxos.

can still see the lower layer of the foundations and some fragments of a frieze in relief with plant mo-

tifs. It has not been possible to ascertain to which divinity the Temple was dedicated

In Naxos, the most important divinities worshipped were Dionysus, who even appeared on the coins minted in the town, and Apollo archegétes (architect). It is also known that the town dedicated a large sanctuary to Aphrodite but this has yet to be discovered. To the south of the Temple there is an altar from the 6th century BC and two kilns dating from the same period, used by the Sanctuary for producing votive statues and architectural decorations. Numerous other kilns have been found, mostly outside the walls. At the end of the 6th century BC the town was completely surrounded by defensive megalithic walls, made of lava stone, with four gates: two long stretches of these walls can be seen in the south-western corner of the site, with two gates opening towards the sea. This period also saw the first coins minted in Naxos: they depict the effigy of Dionysus on one side and a bunch of grapes on the other. In the following century the bunch of grapes was replaced by a Silenus.

In the 5th century BC the town had a geometrical orthogonal layout with three main streets laid out in an east-west direction (platéiai), the central one being wider than the others, and numerous streets laid out in a north-south direction (stenopòi), 39 metres from one another, which cross the plateiai and create rectangular 'blocks'. Two districts that housed potters have also been identified, very near the walls, where masks, decorations for buildings

and pottery were produced.

In the classical age another Necropolis was used, a Necropolis which was a long way from the town, unlike the northern one. In this second Necropolis about one hundred tombs have been found to the west of the Santa Venera river. The archaeological area is open to visitors every day from 9 a.m. until one hour before sunset.

The Archaeological Museum

At the very tip of the Schisò promontory, housed in a 17th century fort, stands the **Archaeological Museum**, an integral part of the Archaeological Park of the ancient town of Naxos.

Most of the exhibits on display in the Museum were found during the various digs carried out in Naxos and date from the age of the Greek colony and from previous occupations of the site in prehistoric and protohistoric times.

On the **ground floor** you can see exhibits illustrating the urban development of Naxos and the most important phases in its history. The display cases contain pieces of pottery dating back to the archaic era of the town; pieces of pottery from the Neolithic period and, in particular, numerous pieces from the Bronze Age.

Of particular interest are the **two *pithoi*** (containers for foodstuffs) uncovered in the *thémenos* area, near the mouth of the Santa Venera river, and used as funeral urns.

On the upper floor you will find exhibits illustrating the life of the town from its birth until the Byzantine period.

There are two rooms containing material uncovered in the town, the necropolises and the sacred areas.

In the first room there are numerous pieces of decorative material from cellae: fictile slabs with coloured decoration, antefixes with Silenus heads, a piece of a sphinx.

In particular, there is a fragment of painted eaves, with plant motif decoration in relief, and a **fictile arula**, called Heidelberg-Naxos, with two symmetrical sphinxes and a central ornamental motif.

This artefact was reconstructed thanks to the archaeologist Paola Pelegatti, who discovered one of the two fragments of which the arula is composed in the Museum of the University of Heidelberg. You can also see prints and left over pieces of pottery found near the kilns.

In the **second room** exhibits on display include everyday objects and funereal objects, a **statuette of a goddess** dating from the 5th century BC portraying Hera and pottery, both locally produced and imported.

The Museum is open to the public every day from 9 a.m. to 2 p.m.

The Gorge
of the Alcàntara River

The Alcàntara river is just under 50km long in all and marks part of the border between the provinces of Catania and Messina. The river rises in the Nebrodi mountains, near Floresta, and flows into the sea near Taormina, crossing the territory of 15 districts in the two provinces.

There is a certain amount of confusion regarding the more ancient names of the river and its identification. We will now explain this better. The Greeks are said to have called it 'akesine', that is 'healing river', but some claim that the Akesine corresponds, in reality, to the Fiumefreddo river.

The Romans are said to have called it 'onabala' or 'onobola', but some believe this was the name of a torrent that has nothing to do with the river in question. The Romans, however, are thought to have built a bridge across the river, something that seems relatively plausible.

Indeed, the Arabs, who always changed the names of the places they conquered according to the characteristics of the place, called the river 'Al Qantarah', which means bridge.

The fame of the Alcàntara, whose water is cold even in summer, is closely tied to the spectacular gorge, which is situated in the province of Messina, a visit that we strongly recommend and which we will deal with later. However, the gorge is only one stretch of the river. Throughout its length, the Alcàntara offers beautiful scenery and luxuriant vegetation, home to numerous species of animals.

At Fondaco Motta (Catania) there are water springs which feed the river in dry periods, indeed the Alcàntara has plenty of water at any time of year.

At Mitogio (Catania) there is a particularly lovely stretch with basalt rocks.

The river can be followed swimming, on foot or by canoe. However, canoeists should pay great attention and not venture out alone, counting on their experience and ability.

The Alcànatra does not have a regular flow, it is often winding and meandering, sometimes it forms small ponds and sometimes quite substantial waterfalls. We therefore underline the concept that **the river is very dangerous for canoeists**. It is a good idea to contact the Acqua Terra Adventure Shop Association (tel. 095 503020), which supplies information, equipment and guides and which has installed hand-ropes and other aids in difficult points to help the passage of canoes.

As we have already said, the most charming stretch of the river and the most interesting from a natural and geological point of view is

the one in the province of Messina, called the Alcàntara **Gorge**. Here the water flows on a gravel bottom and the walls, which are five metres apart, are dark because made of lava.

The area is well equipped from a tourist's point of view. On private land there is a car park, snack bar and a picnic area. A small fee is payable for using the lift that takes you down into the Gorge. Alternatively, you can use the steps, situated about a hundred metres from the car park on the main road. You have to equip yourself with rubber boots, which can be hired on the spot, because at certain points the water is quite deep and the bottom is slippery.

The origin of the walls of the Gorge is clearly linked to a volcanic eruption of long ago, around which a legend has also been created. Once upon a time two brothers, one of whom was blind, had to share out a large amount of grain. Obviously the sighted one divided it, using a 'mojo' (a cylindrical container with a convex bottom). As they say in Sicialian '*cu sparti avi a megghiu parti*' (he who shares out takes the best part) and the sighted one easily deceived his brother, handing him the '*mojo*' filled on the less capacious

side. To the blind one, however, it seemed full when touching it. Needless to say the dishonest one was unable to enjoy the mountain of grain he had accumulated. The grain and the thief were turned into a real mountain, or rather into the volcano Mojo, from which a terrible eruption came forth.

In reality the Alcàntara Gorge is nothing more than the result of an enormous lava flow from Mojo, the most unpredictable secondary crater on Etna.

The flow was made up of basic lava, more fluid than acidic lava and slower to solidify. It flowed along the Alcàntara, blocking the

river, and reached the sea, where it created the small peninsula of Capo Schisò.

The peculiarity of the Gorge is due to the fact that water erosion over the centuries has revealed the internal conformation of the thick basalt walls. They have a column structure with hexagonal and pentagonal prisms that are mostly perpendicular to the height of the walls. This geological phenomenon is determined by the cooling of the lava, which begins externally and gradually reaches the interior. The Alcàntara Gorge is one of the most spectacular examples of this phenomenon in Europe.

Etna: the Volcano

Etna is the most majestic active volcano in Europe, the highest mountain in Sicily. Its presence is worrying, frightening, fascinating and seductive. It is typical of human nature to be able to dedicate to the same object both love and hatred at the same time.

Indeed, Sicilian people love and hate Etna, they submit to the charm of such a magnificent presence, they are proud of their regional park and of their mountain of fire, but they know that it could destroy them, that lava flows quickly. Yet, none of them would really like the activity of the volcano to end.

The lava of Etna is present just about everywhere, in the city and the towns, in the cliffs and the hills, in the church facades and lying alongside the road.

The colour of lava is dominant and even the local produce takes on this colour: cauliflowers and 'tarocchi' (a variety of orange).

Living with the volcano is now almost part of the genetic make-up of the people of Catania. Etna is not a mountain isolated by its height of over 3,300 metres (12,400 feet), it is not a volcano that makes its presence felt only when in full eruption.

Everybody here (from Giarre to Bronte, from Randazzo to Misterbianco) is accustomed to wiping the black sand of Etna from their cars, doing the washing again because the clothes hung out to dry have been stained with black ash, putting up with the earth tremors, sometimes slight at others more serious, that accompany the changing moods of the mountain, of not trusting the clouds in the sky, which might not be what they seem but smoke from Etna. There is a certain amount of fatalism in all this, an ancient fatalism that has often gone hand in hand with faith, superstition, myth and legend.

What can be done against the unbridled forces of nature? Today scientists keep a watchful eye on Etna and are able to foresee activity, both great and small. Today technicians have the means at their disposal to try to divert the direction of lava flows.

Yet, now as in the past, people invoke patron Saints to protect the towns from the lava and the eruptions. While scientists busy themselves with lasers and highly sophisticated equipment, people continue to carry relics and simulacrums in procession to defeat the beloved-detested mountain of fire.

So every town has its heavenly champion in the fight against Etna. In Fornazzo the heavy responsibility lies with the Sacred Heart of Jesus, in Nicolosi with Saint Anthony, in Catania with the veil of Saint Agatha.

However, like all important natural phenomena, over the centuries Etna has not only aroused all kinds of emotion in the population, generating fear, veneration, amazement, legends. It has also

aroused the interest of scientists and researchers, of travellers (especially in the Romantic period) fascinated by its beauty and its terrible majesty and has inspired poets and writers, such as Hesiod, Pindar, Virgil and Dante. It is perhaps Virgil, in the third book of the Aeneid, who left us the most lyrical and effective description of Etna.

"The port, sheltered from the winds, is large and tranquil;/ but up above Etna thunders with frightening shudders,/ and occasionally throws up, black, a cloud into the air/ dense vortices and smoking burning sparks,/ and sends up sheets of flame touching the stars./ Sometimes pieces of rock, from the bowels of the mountain,/ are thrown out by the eruption, and liquefied rocks amass with roars/ boil up from below./ It is said that the body of Enceladus, half burnt by lightning,/ lies under this mass, and above giant Etna/ weighs down on him and puffs out the flames through cracks and chimneys./ And every time it moves its tired side, it shakes the whole/ of Trinacria and thunders, filling the sky with smoke".

Bottom: excursion to the central crater on the summit.

Virgil refers to the myth of Enceladus, one of the giants that rebelled against Jupiter. The father of the gods punished him by striking him with lightning and throwing him against Etna, under which he remained imprisoned. The eruptions are the puffs of his body in flames.

There are two more mythological stories connected with the mountain. Another giant, Typheus, who

had tried to climb up to heaven, was segregated by Jupiter in the mountain. The furious giant vomits flames and fire.

Finally, in the bowels of the mountain is Vulcan's black forge, in which the Cyclops worked making lightning.

Top: beach, boats and volcano.

The name of the volcano comes from the Phoenician 'attano' (furnace) or the Greek 'aitho' (burning) to which is also connected the Latin 'Aetna'

The Arabs called it 'Gibel Utlamat', in other words mountain of fire. Some sources, dating from around 1000 already use the name 'Mons Gibel', then changed into 'Mongibello' (Dante, in the 1200s, also used this name in the 15th canto of Hell).

Etna was formed about 500,000 years ago. The scientific explanation of its birth is directly connected to the phenomenon of continental drift and particularly to the colossal clash between the African and Eurasian shelves, the same clash that probably caused the creation of the Alps and the Himalayas.

The immense impact between the two shelves caused the compression of the magma that was deep below the sea and it came out violently, creating Etna.

Obviously, over thousands of years, the mountain has undergone considerable transformations and, although today its geological history can be partly reconstructed, as regards the relationship between

the volcano and man, the history of Etna is still fundamentally based on myths and the most important eruptions, even though the number of eruptions recorded is certainly much lower than the real number.

Several centuries before Christ there are already references to the activity of the volcano in historical sources. Two important eruptions were those of 475 BC and 396 BC.

From the end of the 1st century AD onwards more eruptions are documented, about 200 up to the present day.

One of the most serious happened in 1669.

Top: a mountain of lava envelops farmhouses and crops.

The volcanic activity was preceded and accompanied by strong earth tremors, new eruptive mouths opened up, some of which created the Monti Rossi behind Nicolosi, and the lava almost completely devastated Catania and Nicolosi in just 18 days.

Another eruption with catastrophic effects was the one in 1811, which particularly affected the Bove Valley, where a new crater was formed.

The activity of 1843 was terrible. Running downhill, the lava crossed an area of marshland and, on contact with the damp ground, created tremendous ex-

plosions that killed several people.

There was a violent eruption in 1866, which created the crater of Monte Gemmellaro.

The eruption of 1892 was longer and more serious, forming the craters of the Monti Silvestri.

In the 20th century there have been numerous eruptions: in 1910, 1928, 1950 (the activity began in March and continued until the December of the following year, 372 days, during which the lava caused enormous damage overrunning vineyards, orchards, grazing land, broom thickets), 1952, 1971 (when the observatory and the cable car were destroyed), 1979 (when nine people were killed by the sudden expulsion of a lava plug from an eruptive mouth), 1983 (the lava damaged the Sapienza mountain hut and the lower cable car station) and in 1992 (the year that saw people all over Italy following with apprehension the news about the lava that was threatening the town of Zafferana).

Top: a river of lava.

Bottom: a spectacular eruption.

The last two dates are worthy of particular attention because on both occasions attempts were made to put an end to the atavistic fatalism of the local people faced by eruptions by trying to divert the lava flow with explosives, with partial success, in order to save the threatened towns. On 13th July 2001 spectacular eruptions with rivers of lava reached the Sapienza Mountain Hut, destroying the ski lifts.

In October 2002 a one kilometre long crack opened up with eruptions and lava flows that ran downhill both on the southern slopes and towards Piano Provenzana, below the two thousand metre mark (two months of continuous eruptions).

The landscape of the Catania area is greatly influenced by the presence of Etna, which is visible even from a great distance.

It occupies a vast area of the province, indeed its circumference at the base is about 250 km.

Even though it is an old volcano, constantly active, numerous towns have grown up on its slopes, divided, in a certain sense, by the mass of the mountain, which is, as we have already said, over 3,300 metres high (even though its height, like its appearance, can change depending on the volcanic activity, which creates small cones, craters etc.).

It is true to say that life revolves around the foot of the mountain, so much so that the towns here are connected by the famous Circumetnea railway, opened at the end of the 19th century.

It could be said that each town has its 'own' volcano.

Indeed, the appearance of the mountain changes according to the place from which it is viewed. So the Etna you see from Sant'Alfio is different from the one seen from Linguglossa, the one seen from Randazzo is different from the one you see from Adrano, and so on.

Bottom: detail of the 1999 eruption.

The continuous eruptions and lava flows over the centuries have not only created outright hills and mountains but also characteristic formations, closely linked to the process of magma consolidation.

Some of these formations are called dykes, daggers (open spaces), the Crags of Acitrezza are nothing more than a rocky agglomerate that came

from an eruption. The lava of Etna is particularly fluid (the temperature of the magma is about 1,000°C), which brings both advantages and disadvantages.

The fluidity means that gases escape more easily, reducing the risk of explosions.

However, fluidity also means speed; the lava flows quickly and can cover great distances in a short time.

It is the latter characteristic that makes Etna a seriously dangerous volcano because the rapidity of its lava flows make it more difficult to organise appropriate action to divert the flows and defend the towns.

Overall it can be said that Etna is rather moderate as regards explosions and expulsion of lava and lapilli.

This is due to the fact that every day it gives off tons of gases and sulphur dioxide into the air (looking like clouds from afar), maintaining an acceptable level of internal pressure.

Obviously, however, pressure builds up to an explosion when lava plugs are created, blocking the eruptive mouths.

Etna has four summit eruptive craters (New Crater, Central Crater, South Eastern Crater and North Eastern Crater) and numerous lateral craters.

The Etna Regional Nature Park was set up in 1987, covers 60,000 hectares and includes 20 district councils of the province of Catania.

No form of life, vegetable or animal, is present in the areas affected by recent lava flows, while the areas of old lava flows are teeming with life.

The flora numbers over 1,500 species, including the soapwort, symbol of the Park, and the fauna counts numerous species of mammals and birds.

The natural landscape changes according to the altitude.

At sea-level, along the coast, the vegetation is mostly halphilous. As you begin to climb up, you find land given over to growing apples, citrus fruits, pears, nuts, pistachios, almonds and, naturally, grapes.

These gradually give way to pinewoods, ilex groves, oak woods and chestnut woods.

From 1,500 to 2,000 metres the landscape is dom-

Top: springtime view of Etna.

Facing page: Monti Silvestri.

inated by beech-trees, aetnesis birches and large fragrant gorse bushes. Above 2,000 metres you only find extremely hardy plants, such as groundsel and mouse-ear chickweed.

The fauna is also very interesting.

On Etna you can find porcupines, foxes, wild rabbits, wild cats, hedgehogs, dormice and, pay attention, vipers.

The birds, above all, give particular joy to animal observers and especially to birdwatchers.

The Park is populated by both diurnal and nocturnal birds.

These include Golden Eagles, Peregrine Falcons, Kestrels, Rock Partridges, Scops Owls, Buzzards, Barn Owls, Cuckoos and Tawny Owls.

In the Gurrida lake you can also see ducks, herons and other aquatic species.

Although the Park can be visited freely and independently, we recommend visitors take the greatest care, especially when hiking.

You do not need special equipment, just hiking boots, a map, binoculars and, obviously, a camera.

Nicolosi: the gateway to Etna

For once history leaves no space for doubt and interpretation: from the 18th century until the early 20th century the only access to the volcano was from Nicolosi. Only here, from the 1700s onwards, were there local people able to place their services at the disposal of travelling aristocrats and to take them up to the summit.

Finally, in 1936 the long awaited moment arrived when the road up Etna was opened. A long series of hairpin bends up to an altitude of 1,900 metres, the road changed attitudes to the volcano. No more tiring mule-back climbs, but fast drives up in motor vehicles, which began to carry up tourists to the edge of the desert area. The 1936 road was destroyed by the 1983 lava flow but has been worthily replaced by a lovely provincial road that largely follows the same route and twists its way gently up the slope of the volcano as far as the Etna-south tourist area. From here there is an efficient transport service by means of cable car and off-road vehicles in order to get up near the summit, at the Philosopher's Tower (2,920 metres). If you prefer to climb up on foot, you can follow the same route taken by the off-road vehicles (see the description of the fourth itinerary of the Cross-Etna Walk) calculating about three and a half hours of walking to reach the Philosopher's Tower. Near the Sapienza mountain hut you can also make a short excursion to the summit of the nearby Monti Silvestri (the first craters you see from the cable car station looking east) formed at the end of the 19th century, or you can go down towards Piano Vetore (heading for the Etna Grand Hotel) and then go up the mount of the same name (accessible along convenient forest paths, 1,820 metres) from which you enjoy a lovely view both towards the summit craters and towards the coast.

Giuseppe Riggio and Giuseppe Vitali

Shopping and leisure time

Nothing could be easier or more pleasurable than buying a souvenir in one of the numerous shops situated in the town centre, especially along the main street Corso Umberto. Whether you are  looking for something to remember your holiday by or a present to take back to friends or relatives at home, the choice is so wide and varied that you will wish you had a bigger suitcase. You will be tempted by the beautiful pottery, both local and from other parts of Sicily, made using both traditional and modern methods, in either delicate or bright colours. If you are worried about pottery breaking in your luggage and would prefer something more robust, you can buy one of the many objects made with inlaid stone or some handmade jewellery. Finally, if you want to buy something for your home, take back some of the patiently and expertly made lacework or an antique print to hang on the wall. All year round Taormina plays host to a whole series of cultural and artistic events, concerts and shows, which will make your  stay here even more enjoyable and memorable. Apart from the traditional religious feast days – such as the celebrations in honour of the patron Saint of the town, Saint Pancras, with a procession through the streets on 9th July – and the carnival, the most important event of the year is Taormina Arte. In truth the various concerts, plays, operas and films that make up this event are held all year round, but the highpoint is the prestigious Film Fes-

On these pages, a few of the countless shops in Corso Umberto.

tival, hosting films from all over the world, which are shown in the beautiful setting of the Greek Theatre. With excursions, swimming and sunbathing, sightseeing and shopping you will probably have little time left for anything else. Taormina, however, has plenty more to offer you in terms of entertainment and leisure. One of the favourite pastimes for both locals and tourists alike is sitting outside one of the many bars in Corso Umberto or Piazza IX Aprile and watching the world go by with a cold drink or a delicious icecream in their hand. Among the numerous bars we recommend the Mocambo, with its lively atmosphere, and the Wunderbar, if you prefer somewhere a little more refined and romantic, both of which are in Piazza IX Aprile. For intellectuals, we suggest Intramoenia, in via De Spuches.

Later on, in the evening, there are plenty of discotheques and night-clubs ready to welcome night owls of all ages. We recom-

mend Marabù, in Giardini-Naxos, one of the most popular; the piano-bar La Giara. In the summer Tout Va and Septimo offer you the chance to enjoy your music in the open air, since they both have beautiful gardens.

Sooner or later you will want to sleep: you will be spoilt for choice by the hotel accommodation on offer in Taormina and

along the coast. There is something for everyone, satisfying all possible tastes and budgets, ranging from large luxurious hotels to small family-run guest houses, set in beautiful gardens or right on the beach, often housed in buildings of great historical importance and architectural beauty.

Taormina Cuisine: paradise of the senses

Taormina cuisine is largely similar to traditional Sicilian cuisine, meaning that even the simplest dish is something delicious to be savoured and not rushed: durum wheat pasta delicious fish and meat, exquisite vegetables and fruit.

These represent a great wealth of traditions that have been absorbed over the centuries, thanks to the various invaders and conquerors, each of whom have left something behind in Sicily.

It is as if somebody had mixed together in a pot all the peculiarities of Arab, French, Norman, Spanish and Bourbon cuisine, in a sort of magical rite, adding a pinch of a secret ingredient so that all the different flavours mix in a harmonious way.

Thus, you can taste the warm climate, the 'burning' sun, the 'scorched' earth, the forces of nature that have been so kind to Sicily.

As if that weren't enough, the large number of restaurants in Taormina (more than 80) means that this cuisine is subject to an infinite number of variations.

The dishes on offer are simple, refined and tasty, famous all over the world, but only here can you experience them in such a unique setting, heightening the whole experience.

If you travel to Sicily, take the chance to enjoy a full meal, composed of starters, first and second courses, dessert and fruit. You will find that, despite the huge quantity of food you will be served, the meal will be tasty, light and healthy, since Mediterranean cuisine does not use fats, except for olive oil, or other ingredients that can damage your health.

Tuck in then and try the seafood starters, which are delicious in Taormina, Italian style starters (with ham, salami, olives, aubergines, pickled vegetables), "caponata", "peperonata" and vegetables.

Then continue with the wide variety of first courses, ranging from simple pasta in tomato sauce to the richer dishes such as pennette "alla catanese", or pasta "alla Norma", delicious pasta with sardines or delicate linguine in lemon.

You then move on to the second course of meat (sausage, rabbit, goat...) or fish (swordfish, sardines, mullet, stockfish...), washing it all down with some good local wine or, if you prefer something more refined, a bottle of Corvo, Rapitalà, Regaleali... You finish off with a typical Sicilian dessert (cannoli, cassata, lemon cake).

At the end of the evening you will probably be "tired, but happy!"

PASTA "ALLA NORMA"

Ingredients: 320g of pasta (preferably perciatelli) - 500g of fresh tomato – a few leaves of basil - 3 aubergines - 2 cloves of garlic - 1 spoonful of salted ricotta – extra virgin olive oil – salt and pepper.

Wash the aubergines, cut them into small pieces and lightly fry in a non-stick pan with olive oil.
Then finish cooking them in the oven in a metal baking tray lightly greased with oil.

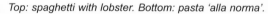

Top: spaghetti with lobster. Bottom: pasta 'alla norma'.

Lightly fry the cloves of garlic in the same oil used for the aubergines, add the fresh tomato pulp and cook on a medium heat for a few minutes.

When cooked, remove the garlic and add chopped basil, salt and pepper.

In the meantime cook the perciatelli in plenty of salted water, drain and mix with the tomato sauce. Serve after sprinkling the pasta with the pieces of aubergine and grated ricotta.

STOCKFISH "A GHIOTTA"

Ingredients: stockfish - flour - potatoes - capers - onion - pepper - salt – black olives – olive oil

Cut the stockfish into pieces and put them into soak. First lightly fry the onion and then the pieces of stockfish dipped in flour; then add a little water, the potatoes cut into small pieces, the capers, the pepper and just a pinch of salt.

Cook on a low heat and add the black olives only when nearly cooked.

Bottom: in Taormina... even cats lick their lips.

RABBIT "ALLA SICILIANA"

Ingredients: 1 rabbit weighing about 1.2kg – onion – celery – carrot – rosemary – laurel – sage – full-bodied red wine – wine vinegar – sugar – 50g of pine seeds – 30g of butter – olive oil – salt and peppercorns

Clean the rabbit, wash it and dry. Then cut it into pieces and place in a baking tray

In a pan bring to the boil half a litre of red wine, flavoured with a laurel leaf, two sage leaves, a twig of rosemary, half an onion, half a stick of celery, a carrot and a few peppercorns. Remove the pan from the heat and, when the liquid is almost cold, pour it onto the rabbit and leave it to marinate for at least six hours. At the end of this time drain it. In another pan melt some butter and add three spoonfuls of oil, then use this to brown a finely chopped onion and add the pieces of rabbit.

Brown and add salt and a few spoonfuls of the marinated liquid drained previously.

As the rabbit cooks, add this liquid a little at a time as needed so that the rabbit doesn't dry.

Just before removing the rabbit from the heat, mix three spoonfuls of vinegar and a spoonful of sugar in a small pan over a low heat. When this mixture has turned yellowish, add the pine seeds and sultanas softened in warm water and squeezed. Mix and pour over the rabbit.

Let the flavours mix for a few minutes and then serve your rabbit "alla siciliana".

SICILIAN CANNOLI

Ingredients: for the shells: 250g of flour - 25g of lard - 50g of sugar – a little red wine – salt
For the filling: 500g of ricotta – plain chocolate – icing sugar - 1/2 sachet of vanilla – candied orange
Preparation time: 50 m.

If you are not a particularly good cook, or if you want to save time, you can buy the cannoli shells in the supermarket (make sure they are crumbly and not too hard).

If you have the time and the ability we advise you to make them yourselves. Get hold of some tubes (which are made either of cane or of metal), around which the pastry is wrapped. The evening before mix together the flour, lard, sugar and a pinch of salt, adding also a little wine to keep the pastry soft. Wrap the mixture in a cloth and put it in the fridge overnight.

The next day roll out the pastry and cut into squares of 10 centimetres, fairly thin, taking care not to break the pastry. Wrap the squares of pastry around the tubes, starting from the corner of each square. Fry them one by one in very hot oil, taking care to make them golden brown but not to burn them. Then allow them to cool and remove them carefully. You can now move on to the preparation of the filling.

"Beat" the ricotta with the sugar in a mixing bowl and sift twice. Add the plain chocolate cut into very small squares and the pieces of candied orange.

Use this cream to fill the cannoli, lay them on a plate, sprinkle with icing sugar and place a slice of candied orange at each end of the cannoli (alternatively, you can decorate the ends with chopped pistachios).

SICILIAN CASSATA

Ingredients: a 500g sponge cake – rum - 400g of ricotta - 200g of icing sugar - 250g of candied fruit
100g of plain chocolate - 200g of granulated sugar – vanilla powder
Preparation time: 60 minutes.

"Beat" the ricotta with the sugar in a mixing bowl and sift twice. Add 200 grams of candied fruit, the chocolate cut into small pieces and a pinch of vanilla.

Cover a high sided cake dish with one of the thick layers of sponge cake and fill the centre with the ricotta mixture.

Cover with another layer of sponge cake and place in the fridge for a few hours. Use the granulated sugar to make the icing and when it is ready pour it over the cassata on a cake platter. Garnish with pieces of candied fruit.

* The icing is made boiling 200g of sugar in half a glass of water. You will know it is ready when it forms a string between your fingers. At this point pour it onto a worktop and beat with a wooden spatula until it turns white.

RICE "CRISPELLE"

Ingredients: 1kg of rice – half a litre of milk - 300g of sugar – cinnamon – lemon peel – flour – vegetable oil - honey

Boil the rice (without adding salt) and, once cooked, drain and put back into the saucepan with the milk, a little cinnamon, the sugar and grated lemon peel.

Remove from heat when the rice has absorbed all the milk. Allow to cool and prepare the "crispelle", moulding the rice into a stick shape.

Dip them in the flour and fry in plenty of hot vegetable oil (don't let them get too crisp).

Once cooked dip them into the honey and sprinkle with ground cinnamon.

If preferred, the "crispelle" can be dipped into sugar rather then honey.

Vincenzo Giusto

Where to eat in Taormina

RESTAURANTS

- A MASSARIA: Via Arancio, 6. Tel. 0942 50243.
- A ZAMMARA: Via F.lli Bandiera, 15. Tel. 0942 24408.
- AL CASTELLO: Via Madonna Della Rocca, 9/A. Tel. 0942 28158.
- AL DUOMO: Vico Ebrei/Piazza Duomo. Tel. 0942 625656.
- AL FEUDO: Contrada Coniglio Feo. Tel. 0942 58042.
- AL GIARDINO: Via Bagnoli Croci, 84. Tel. 0942 23453.
- AL SARACENO: Via Madonna Della Rocca, 16. Tel. 0942 632015.
- BOUGAINVILLE: Via Bagnoli Croce, 88. Tel. 0942 625218.
- CICLOPE: Corso Umberto. Tel. 0942 23263.
- DA LORENZO: Via Roma, 12. Tel. 0942 23480.
- DA MAFFEI: Via San Domenico de Guzman, 1. Tel. 0942 24055.
- DA SARO: Via Costantino Patricio, 24. Tel. 0942 23934.
- GRANDUCA: Corso Umberto, 172. Tel. 0942 24983.
- GROTTA AZZURRA: Via Bagnoli Croci, 2. Tel. 0942 24163.
- IL BORGHETTO: Salita Celestino Penna, 5. Tel. 0942 626062.
- LA GIARA: Vico La Floresta, 1. Tel. 0942 23360.
- L'ARCO DEI CAPPUCCINI: Via Cappuccini. Tel. 0942 24893.
- L'OROLOGIO: Via San Giovanni Bosco, 37/A. Tel. 0942 625572.
- LA BOTTE: Piazza San Domenico 3/4. Tel. 0942 24198.
- LA BUCA: Corso Umberto, 140. Tel. 0942 24314.
- LA DRACENA: Via Michele Amari, 4. Tel. 0942 23491.
- LA PIAZZETTA: Vico Paladini, 5/7. Tel. 0942 626317.
- LA VENERE: Piazza S. Antonio. Tel. 0942 23367.
- LE ARCATE: Via Giardinazzo,8. Tel. 0942 625766.
- LURALEO: Via Bagnoli Croce, 27. Tel. 0942 24279.
- RISTORANTE LA GRIGLIA: Corso Umberto, 54. Tel. 0942 23980.
- ROSTICEPI: Via San Pancrazio, 18. Tel. 0942 24149.
- SEPTIMO: Via San Pancrazio, 50. Tel. 0942 625522.
- TERRAZZA ANGELO: Corso Umberto, 38. Tel. 0942 24411.
- TIRAMISÙ: Via C.Patricio,10 (Porta Messina). Tel. 0942 24165.
- TOUT VA: Via Luigi Pirandello, 70. Tel. 0942 23824.
- U BOSSU: Via Bagnoli Croce, 50. Tel. 0942 23311.
- VICOLO STRETTO: Via Vicolo Stretto, 6. Tel. 0942 23849.
- VILLA SIRINA: C/o Hotel Villa Sirina, Via Sirina.

TRATTORIAS

- TAVERNA AL PALADINO: Via Naumachia, 21. Tel. 0942 24614.
- TAVERNA BURRASCA: Via D'Orville, 6. Tel. 0942 2404.
- COSÌ È SE VI PIACE: Piazza San Pancrazio. Tel. 0942 24743
- DA NINO: Via Luigi Pirandello, 37a. Tel. 0942 21265.
- DON CAMILLO: Via C. Ottaviano, 2. Tel. 0942 23198.
- IL BACCANALE: Piazzetta E. Filea. Tel. 0942 625390.
- L'ANFORA: Salita Dente, 1. Tel. 0942 24647.
- NAUTILUS: Via San Pancrazio, 48. Tel. 0942 625024.
- TRATTORIA SICILIANA: Via Ospedale, 9. Tel. 0942 24780.
- U LANTIRNARU: Via Apollo Arcate, 14. Tel. 0942 24565.

The pizzerias include: Aquarius: AQUARIUS: Via Francavilla, 3 . Tel. 0942 50302. BELLA BLU: Via Luigi Pirandello, 28. Tel. 0942 24239. DYONISUS PUB: Via

Cuseni, 5. Tel. 0942 24258. GAMBERO ROSSO: Via Naumachia, 11. Tel. 0942 24863. HOSTARIA DA PEPPE: Via Calapitrulli, 3. Tel. 0942 625359. IL LEONE: Via Bagnoli Croce, 126. Tel. 0942 23878. INN PIERO: Via Luigi Pirandello, 20. Tel. 0942 23139. L'ANGOLO: Via Damiano Rosso, 17. Tel. 0942 625202. LA CIOCIARA: Via Cesare Ottaviano, 1/A. Tel. 0942 24881. LA GINESTRA: Contrada Fontanella. Tel. 0942 62575. LA TRATTORIA: Via Apollo Arcageta, 6. Tel. 0942 23239. LIOLÀ: Via Apollo Arcageta, 9. Tel. 0942 21160. MAMMA ROSA: Via Naumachia, 10. Tel. 0942 24361. PORTA MESSINA: L.go Giove Serapide,4. Tel 0942 23205. PUB MIRAGE: Via Roma, 11. Tel. 0942 24660. SAN PANCRAZIO: Via San Pancrazio, 3. Tel. 0942 23184. TAORMINA: Vico Teofane Cerameo. Tel. 0942 24359. TRATTORIA ANTONIO: Via Crocefisso. Tel. 0942 24570. TROCADERO: Via Luigi Pirandello, 1. Tel. 0942 24330.

Taormina Beach

- ARCO ROSSO: Via Lungomare Mazzeo, 27. Tel. 0942 36601.
- DA CONCETTA: Via Minghetti, 22. Tel. 0942 36689.
- DA GIOVANNI: Via Nazionale - Isolabella. Tel. 0942 23531.
- GAMBERO ROSSO BEACH: Via Nazionale - Contr. Spisone. Tel. 0942 626247.
- IL BARCAIOLO: Spiaggia Mazzarò. Tel. 0942 625633.
- IL CANTONE DEL FARO: Via Sirina, 2. Tel. 0942 56832.
- IL DELFINO: Via Nazionale - Mazzarò. Tel. 0942 23004.
- IL FICODINDIA: Via Appiano - Mazzeo. Tel. 0942 36301.
- IL GABBIANO: Via Nazionale, 202 - Mazzarò. Tel. 0942 625128.
- IL PESCATORE: Via Nazionale, 107. Tel. 0942 23460.
- LA BUSSOLA: Via Nazionale - Isola Bella. Tel. 0942 21276.
- LA CARAVELLA: Contr. Spisone. Tel. 0942 24269.
- LA RAMPA: Via Nazionale - Contr. Mazzarò, 196/a. Tel. 0942 24212.
- LIDO CAPARENA: c/oHotel Lido Caparena, Via Nazionale, 189. Tel. 0942 652033.

- LIDO COPACABANA: Lungomare Mazzeo. Tel. 0942 36268.
- LIDO LA DOLCE VITA: Contr. Spisone, 1. Tel. 0942 24056.
- LIDO LA PIGNA: Via Nazionale - Mazzarò. Tel. 0942 21276.
- LIDO MAZZEO: Via Lungomare, 27. Tel. 0942 36075.
- LIDO MENDOLIA CLUB: Isola Bella. Tel. 0942 625258.
- LIDO MERIDIEN: Via Nazionale - Spisone. Tel. 0942 23170.
- LIDO RE DEL SOLE: Via Nazionale - Spisone. Tel. 0942 625385.
- LIDO STOCKHOLM: Via Nazionale - Contr. Spisone, 173. Tel. 0942 625195.
- LIDO TROPICANA: Via Lungomare, 27. Tel. 0942 36579.
- OASI: Via Nazionale - Contr. Spisone. Tel. 0942 626247.
- PIZZICHELLA: Spiaggia Isola Bella. Tel. 0942 625189.
- PRINCIPE: c/o Hotel Raneri Principe, Via Nazionale - Mazzarò. Tel. 0942 23962.
- SICILIA BEDDA: Via Appiano - Mazzeo. Tel. 0942 36772.
- VILLA CAGNONE: Via Lungomare. Mazzeo. Tel. 0942 36410.

Castelmola

- BUCALO: Via Madonna della Scala, 4. Tel. 0942 28603.
- CHICCHIRICHÌ: C.da Ogliastrello. Tel. 0942 28021.
- EUROPA: Via Pio IX, 26. Tel. 0942 28481.
- IL MANIERO: Via Salita Castello. Tel. 0942 28180.
- LE MIMOSE: Via Tutti i Santi, 43. Tel. 0942 28216.
- PARCO REALE: Via Porta Mola, 9. Tel. 0942 28082.
- TAVERNA DELL'ETNA: Via A. De Gasperi, 29. Tel. 0942 28868.
- 4 STAGIONI: C.da Pandolfo. Tel. 0942 28613.

Giardini Naxos

- AL FAGIANO: Via Nazionale, 1. Tel. 0942 51880.
- ANGELINA: Via Lungomare Naxos. Tel. 0942 51477.
- ARCOBALENO: Via Lungomare Naxos, 169. Tel. 0942 51067.
- CALYPSO: Via IV Novembre, 267. Tel. 0942 51289.
- EDEN: Via Tevere, 1. Tel. 0942 52203.
- EURO: Via Iannuzzi, 31/c. Tel. 0942 54101.
- GAMBRINUS: Via Tysandros, 6. Tel. 0942 54219.
- GARDEN: Via Lungomare Naxos, 24. Tel. 0942 51502.
- GOLDEN BLUE: Via Calcide Eubea, 10. Tel. 0942 52169.
- IL COVO: Via Stracina, 8. Tel. 0942 54159.
- IL FARAONE: Via Nazionale, 122. Tel. 0942 56156.
- IL PIANETA DELLA PIZZA: Via Vitt. Emanuele, 184. Tel. 0942 52044.
- LA BARONESSA: C.so Umberto, 148. Tel. 0942 628191.
- LA CAMBUSA: Via I. Schisr, 3. Tel. 0942 51437.
- LA CAPANNINA: Via Lungomare Naxos, 181. Tel. 0942 56627. Ristorante e pizzeria.
- LA CONCHIGLIA: Via Lungomare Naxos, 221. Tel. 0942 52777.
- LA LAMPARA: Via Tysandros, 32. Tel. 0942 56424.
- LA LANTERNA: Via Lungomare Naxos. Tel. 0942 51369.
- LA ROMANTICA: Via Lungomare Naxos. Tel. 0942 53077.
- LA SIRENA: Via Lungomare Naxos, 36. Tel. 0942 51853.
- LA SPELONGA: Via Recanati, 8. Tel. 0942 54146.
- MARABÙ: Via Iannuzzo, 1. Tel. 0942 54076.

- MARE DI NAXOS: Via Tysandros, 88. Tel. 0942 56605.
- MR. ROLL 2 VENERE: Via Iannuzzi, 31. Tel. 0942 653087.
- NETTUNO: Lungomare Tysandros, 68. Tel. 0942 571276.
- ORPHEUS: Via Calcide Eubea, 3. Tel. 0942 51778.
- PIZZA ORIGANO: Via Vitt. Emanuele, 49/g. Tel. 0942 51685.
- PORTO AZZURRO: Via Calcide Eubea, 8. Tel. 0942 53303.
- POZZO GRECO: Via Lipari, 20. Tel. 0942 56245.
- RENDEZ VOUS: Via Lungomare Naxos, 2. Tel. 0942 52172.
- SABBIE D'ORO: Via Lungomare Naxos, 14. Tel. 0942 52380.
- SANDOKAN: Via Recanati, 2. Tel. 0942 54125.
- SEA SOUND: Via Iannuzzo, 37/a. Tel. 0942 54330.
- SICILIANO: Via Tysandros, 68. Tel. 0942 571276.
- SILIGATO: Via Lungomare Naxos, 215. Tel. 0942 571357.
- SPIZZICO 2: Via Consolare Valeria, 16. Tel. 0942 52167.
- TAVERNA NAXOS: Via Tysandros, 108. Tel. 0942 52251.
- VALENTINO: Via Iannuzzo, 22. Tel. 0942 54203.

Letojanni

- DA CORTESE: Via Nazionale, 3. Tel. 0942 36337.
- DA NINO: Via Luigi Rizzo, 29. Tel. 0942 36147 - 651060.
- DA VICTOR: Via Luigi Rizzo, 45. Tel. 0942 651107.
- IL CORSARO: Via Sillemi, 7/9. Tel. 0942 36570.
- IL FICODINDIA: Via Appiano, 9 (Mazzeo). Tel. 0942 236301.
- LA CAMPAGNOLA: C.da Spezzamartino. Tel. 0942 36851.
- LA FORNACE: Via Michelangelo Garufi, 25. Tel. 0942 36622.
- LAGANÀ: Via Luigi Rizzo, 29. Tel. 0942 36416.
- MEZZA LUNA: Via Luigi Rizzo, 48. Tel. 0942 37020.
- TRIMARCHI: Via Luigi Rizzo, 25. Tel. 0942 37434 - 37341.
- VILLA CAGNONE: Lungomare Mazzeo. Tel. 0942 36410.

Sant'Alessio

- A LAMPARA: Via Madonna del Carmelo, 4. Tel. 0942 750600.
- MIANO F.LLI: Via Nazionale, 89. Tel. 0942 751415.
- PARCO DUCALE: C.da Mantineo. Tel. 0942 751471.
- S. GIUSEPPE: Via Nazionale, 7/a. Tel. 0942 751401.
- TROCADERO: Via Nazionale, 18. Tel. 0942 750777.

Where to stay in Taormina

HOTELS
- GRAND HOTEL TIMEO E VILLA FLORA ♥♥♥♥♥L: Tel. 0942 23801 - fax 628501.
- SAN DOMENICO PALACE HOTEL ♥♥♥♥♥: Tel. 0942 613111 - fax 625506.
- BRISTOL PARK ♥♥♥♥: Tel. 0942 23006 - 23007 - fax 24519.
- EXCELSIOR PALACE ♥♥♥♥: Tel. 0942 23975 - fax 23978. www.excelsior-palacetaormina.it.
- GRAND HOTEL MIRAMARE ♥♥♥♥: Tel. 0942 23401/2/3 - fax 626223.
- GRANDE ALBERGO MONTE TAURO ♥♥♥♥: Tel. 0942 24402 - fax 24403.

- HOTEL VILLA DIODORO ♥♥♥♥: Tel. 0942 23312 - fax 23391.
- MEDITERRANÉE ♥♥♥♥: Tel. 0942 23901 - fax 21231.
- VILLA FABBIANO ♥♥♥♥: Tel. 0942 626058 - fax 23732.
- VILLA PARADISO ♥♥♥♥: Tel. 0942 23921-2 - fax 625800.
- ANDROMACO PALACE HOTEL ♥♥♥: Tel. 0942 23834 - fax 24985.
- ARISTON ♥♥♥: Tel. 0942 6190 - fax 619191.
- BEL SOGGIORNO ♥♥♥: Tel. 0942 23342 - fax 626298.
- CONTINENTAL ♥♥♥: Tel. 0942 23805 - fax 23806.
- CUNDARI INN HOTEL ♥♥♥: Tel. 0942 578238 - fax 578268.
- HOTEL DEL CORSO ♥♥♥: Tel. 0942 628698 - fax 629856.
- ISABELLA ♥♥♥: Tel. 0942 23153 - fax 23155.
- SIRIUS ♥♥♥: Tel. 0942 23477 - fax 23208.
- SOLE CASTELLO ♥♥♥: Tel. 0942 28881 - fax 28444.
- VELLO D'ORO ♥♥♥: Tel. 0942 23788-89-90 - fax 626117.
- VILLA BELVEDERE ♥♥♥: Tel. 0942 23791 - fax 625830.
- VILLA FIORITA ♥♥♥: Tel. 0942 24122 - fax 625967.
- VILLA KRISTINA ♥♥♥: Tel. 0942 28366 - fax 28371.
- VILLA RIIS ♥♥♥: Tel. 0942 24875 - fax 626254.
- VILLA S. MICHELE ♥♥♥: Tel. 0942 24327 - fax 24328.
- VILLA SIRINA ♥♥♥: Tel. 0942 51776 - fax 51671.
- ADELE ♥♥: Tel. 0942 23352 - fax 23352.
- ARISTON II ♥♥: Tel. 0942 6190 - fax 619191.
- CONDOR ♥♥: Tel. 0942 23124 - fax 625726.
- CORONA ♥♥: Tel. 0942 23021 - fax 23022.
- ELIOS ♥♥: Tel./fax 0942 23431.
- HOTEL NATALINA ♥♥: Tel. 0942 24928 - fax 625364.
- HOTEL SOLEADO ♥♥: Tel. 0942 24138-625624 - fax 23617.
- HOTEL VICTORIA ♥♥: Tel. 0942 23372-21278 - fax 623567.
- HOTEL VILLA DUCALE ♥♥: Tel. 0942 28153 - fax 28710.
- LA CAMPANELLA ♥♥: Tel. 0942 23381 - fax 625248.
- PALAZZO VECCHIO ♥♥: Tel. 0942 23033 - fax 625104.
- PRESIDENT HOTEL SPLENDID ♥♥: Tel. 0942 23500 - fax 625289.
- RESIDENCE ♥♥: Tel. 0942 23463 - fax 23464.
- RIVIERA ♥♥: Tel. 0942 51191 - fax 52109.
- VILLA CHIARA ♥♥: Tel. 0942 625421 - fax 52109.
- VILLA GAIA ♥♥: Tel. 0942 23185-6232030 - fax 23185.
- VILLA GRETA ♥♥: Tel. 0942 28286-18347 - fax 24360.
- VILLA IGIEA ♥♥: Tel./fax 0942 625275.
- VILLA NETTUNO ♥♥: Tel. 0942 23797 - fax 626035.
- VILLA SCHULER ♥♥: Tel. 0942 23481 - fax 23522.
- CUNDARI ♥: Tel. 0942 53287.
- INN PIERO ♥: Tel. 0942 23139 - fax 23211.
- LA PRORA ♥: Tel./fax 0942 23940.
- LOCANDA DIANA ♥: Tel. 0942 23898.
- LOCANDA MODERNO ♥: Tel. 0942 51017.
- PUGLIA ♥: Tel. 0942 28315.
- SVIZZERA ♥: Tel. 0942 23790 - fax 625906.
- VILLA ASTORIA ♥: Tel./fax 0942 23943.

RESIDENCES
- RESIDENCE TERRA ROSSA: Tel. 0942 24536 - fax 629000.
- VILLA COSTANZA: Tel. 0942 24717 - fax 24554.
- RESIDENCE VILLA GIULIA: Tel. 0942 23312 - fax 23391.

ROOMS FOR RENT
- CAMERE IL LEONE: Tel./fax 0942 23878.
- CASA GRAZIA: Tel./fax 0942 24776.
- IL CANTONE DEL FARO: Tel. 0942 56832.
- IL GLICINE: Tel. 0942 625972 - fax 0942 23112.
- INGEGNERI GIOVANNINA: Tel. 0942 625486.
- ISOCO GUEST HOUSE: Tel./fax 0942 23679.
- RESIDENCE CIRCE: Tel./fax 0942 23168.
- SCHULER: Tel. 0942 24736.
- TRUGLIO MARIA CONCETTA: Tel. 0942 36689.
- VILLA OASIS: Tel. 0942 36510.

FARM HOLIDAYS
- VILLA ANTONELLA: Tel. 0942 654131.
- TERRENIA: Tel./fax 0942 654100.
- LE CASE DEL PRINCIPE: Tel. 0942 577137 - fax 577235.

YOUTH HOSTELS
- TAORMINA'S ODYSSEY: Tel. 0942 24533 - fax 23211.
- ULISSE: Tel./fax 0942 23193.

BED & BREAKFAST
- CORVAIA B&B: Tel. 0942 628808 - fax 625400.
- THE DOLPHINS: Tel. 0942 24892.
- VILLA SARA: Tel. 0942 28138 - fax 02 700544436.

Taormina Beach

HOTELS
- GRAND HOTEL ATLANTIS BAY ♥♥♥♥ L: Tel. 0942 618011 - fax 23194.
- GRAND HOTEL MAZZARÒ SEA PALACE ♥♥♥♥ L: Tel. 0942 612111 - fax 626237.
- CORALLO ♥♥♥♥: Tel. 0942 51510 - fax 51835.
- GRANDE ALBERGO CAPOTAORMINA ♥♥♥♥: Tel. 0942 572111 - fax 625467.
- HOTEL LIDO CAPARENA ♥♥♥♥: Tel. 0942 652033 - fax 36913.
- HOTEL VILLA ESPERIA ♥♥♥♥: Tel. 0942 23377-8 - fax 21105.
- IPANEMA ♥♥♥♥: Tel. 0942 24720-24729 - fax 625821.
- LIDO MEDITERRANÉE ♥♥♥♥: Tel. 0942 24422 - fax 24774.
- PARK HOTEL LA PLAGE ♥♥♥♥: Tel. 0942 626095 - fax 625850.
- VILLA SANT'ANDREA ♥♥♥♥: Tel. 0942 23125 - fax 24838.
- BAIA AZZURRA ♥♥♥: Tel. 0942 23249 - fax 625499.
- BAY PALACE HOTEL ♥♥♥: Tel. 0942 626200 - fax 626199.
- BAIA DELLE SIRENE ♥♥♥: Tel. 0942 628843 - fax 628845.
- HOTEL RANIERI PRINCIPE ♥♥♥: Tel. 0942 23962 - fax 24716.
- IONIC HOTEL MAZZARÒ ♥♥♥: Tel. 0942 23112 - fax 628515.
- ISOLA BELLA ♥♥♥: Tel. 0942 24289 - fax 24288.
- VILLA BIANCA ♥♥♥: Tel. 0942 24488-89 - fax 24832.
- ANTEA ♥♥: Tel. 0942 24933.
- CABLE WAY ♥♥: Tel. 0942 24739 - fax 623119.
- VILLA SOUVENIR ♥♥: Tel./fax 0942 36643.
- VILLA CATERINA ♥♥: Tel./fax 0942 24709.

- VILLINO GALLODORO ♥: Tel./fax 0942 23860.

ROOMS FOR RENT
- TALIO MARIA: Tel./fax 0942 24709.
- VILLAGGIO PLACIDO: Tel. 0942 24754 - fax 625342.

CAMPSITES
- SAN LEO: Tel. 0942 24658.

BED & BREAKFAST
- TAOBAB: Tel./fax 0942 36292.
- VILLA SCHITICCHIU: Tel. 0942 28352 - fax 23568.

Castelmola

- VILLA SONIA ♥♥♥♥: Via Rotabile, 172. Tel. 0942 28082 - fax 28083.
- PANORAMA DI SICILIA ♥♥: Tel./fax 0942 28027.
- VILLA REGINA: Tel. 0942 28228. Rooms for rent.

Giardini Naxos

- ASSINOS PALACE HOTEL ♥♥♥♥: Via Consolare Valeria, 33 (ss. 114). Tel. 0942 576307.
- ATAHOTELS NAXOS BEACH HOTEL ♥♥♥♥: Via Recanati, 26. Tel. 0942 6611.
- CAESAR PALACE ♥♥♥♥: Via Consolare Valeria (ss. 114). Tel. 0942 5590.
- GRANDE ALBERGO CAPOTAORMINA ♥♥♥♥: C.da Recanati. Tel. 0942 576015.
- HELLENIA YACHTING HOTEL ♥♥♥♥: Via Iannuzzi, 41 (Naxos-Schisò). Tel. 0942 54310 - 51737.
- NAXOS BEACH ♥♥♥♥: C.da Recanati. Tel. 0942 5611.
- RAMADA HOTEL ♥♥♥♥: Via Iannuzzi, 47 (Naxos-Schisò). Tel. 0942 51931.
- SANT'ALPHIO GARDEN HOTEL ♥♥♥♥: Via Recanati. Tel. 0942 51383.
- SPORTING BAIA HOTEL ♥♥♥♥: Via Naxos, 6. Tel. 0942 51733.
- TRITONE ♥♥♥♥: Via Tysandros, 22. Tel. 0942 51468.
- ARATHENA ROCKS ♥♥♥: Via Calcide Eubea, 55. Tel. 0942 51349.
- BAIA DEGLI DEI ♥♥♥: C.da Recanati. Tel. 0942 54094.
- KALOS HOTEL ♥♥♥: Via Calcide Eubea, 29. Tel. 0942 52652.
- NIKE HOTEL ♥♥♥: Via C. Eubea, 27. Tel. 0942 51207 - 56314.
- Porto Azzurro ♥♥♥: Via Calcide Eubea, 8. Tel. 0942 571362.
- TOURING ♥♥♥: Via C. Colombo, 8. Tel. 0942 51069.
- ELISEO ♥♥: Via Nazionale, 1. Tel. 0942 52326.
- PALLADIO DR. ♥♥♥: Via IV Novembre, 269. Tel. 0942 52267.
- ALEXANDER: C.da Recanati - Via Iannuzzo, 41. Tel. 0942 54313.
- COSTA AZZURRA: Via Lung. Naxos, 35. Tel. 0942 550457.
- FREE TIME: C.da Cuba. Tel. 0942 571704.
- LA RIVA: Via Tysandros, 52. Tel. 0942 51329.
- PANORAMIC: Via Schisò, 22. Tel. 0942 53466.
- SABBIE D'ORO: Via Lungomare Naxos, 8. Tel. 0942 571362.
- SAN GIOVANNI: Via Umberto, 523. Tel. 0942 51902.
- VILLA NEFELE: Via Vulcano, 2. Tel. 0942 56583.

- VILLA PAMAR: Via Tysandros, 76. Tel. 0942 53069.
- VILLA MORA: Via Lung. Naxos, 47. Tel. 0942 51839. Guest house.
- LA SIRENA: Via Lung. Naxos, 36. Tel. 0942 51853. Guest house.
- OTELLO: Via Tysandros, 62. Tel. 0942 51009. Guest house.
- S. ANTONIO: C.via Filicudi, 8. Tel. 0942 51475. Guest house.
- VILLA GIARDINI: C.via Filicudi, 1. Tel. 0942 52448 - 52805. Guest house.

Letojanni

- ANTARES OLIMPO ♥♥♥♥: Poggio Mastropietro. Tel. 0942 643131 - 6400.
- ALBATROS ♥♥♥: Via Luigi Rizzo. Tel. 0942 37092 - 37287.
- DA PEPPE ♥♥♥: Via Vitt. Emanuele, 345. Tel. 0942 36843.
- BELLATRIX: Poggio Mastropietro. Tel. 0942 640001.
- DELLE PALME: Via dei Vespri, 33. Tel. 0942 36354.
- PARK HOTEL SILEMI: C.da Sillemi. Tel. 0942 6520094.
- S. PIETRO: Via Luigi Rizzo. Tel. 0942 37012.
- EMANUELE: Via Michelangelo Garufi, 31. Tel. 0942 36239. Guest house.
- FERNANDA: Via Roma, 67. Tel. 0942 36261. Guest house.
- LA FORNACE CARMELO: Via Michelangelo Garufi, 25. Tel. 0942 36622. Guest house.

Sant'Alessio

- KENNEDY ♥♥♥: Via Nazionale, 87. Tel. 0942 751110 - 756060.
- ELIHOTEL: Via Lungomare, 274. Tel. 0942 756110.
- LA GROTTA: Via Consolare Valeria, 220. Tel. 0942 750600.
- PAGANO: Via Nazionale, 199. Tel. 0942 751155.
- SOLEMAR: Via Lungomare, 1. Tel. 0942 756137.
- S. GIUSEPPE: Via Nazionale, 7/a. Tel. 0942 751401. Guest house.
- VILLAMARE: Via Lungomare, 5. Tel. 0942 751192. Guest house.

Printed in Mai 2004
by Avvenire 2000 via Area Artigianale, agglomerato ASI
98129 Larderia Inferiore - Messina